Football Workout and Nutrition Journal

This Book Belongs To:

_____

©Red Tiger Press

DATE: [_____] **WEEK:** [____] **WEIGHT:** [_____]

Warm Up/ Stretching		Duration: [_____]

Exercise		Set 1	Set 2	Set 3	Set 4	Set 5
	Weight					
	Reps					
	Weight					
	Reps					
	Weight					
	Reps					
	Weight					
	Reps					
	Weight					
	Reps					
	Weight					
	Reps					
	Weight					
	Reps					
	Weight					
	Reps					
	Weight					
	Reps					
	Weight					
	Reps					
	Weight					
	Reps					
	Weight					
	Reps					
	Weight					
	Reps					

CARDIO WORKOUT

Exercise	Duration	Pace	Heart Rate	Calories

Notes:

DAILY CALORIE TARGET: [ ]

BREAKFAST	Protein	Carbs	Fat	Fiber	Sodium	Calories

SNACK	Protein	Carbs	Fat	Fiber	Sodium	Calories

LUNCH	Protein	Carbs	Fat	Fiber	Sodium	Calories

SNACK	Protein	Carbs	Fat	Fiber	Sodium	Calories

DINNER	Protein	Carbs	Fat	Fiber	Sodium	Calories

SNACK	Protein	Carbs	Fat	Fiber	Sodium	Calories

DAILY TOTALS						
DAILY GOALS						
% DAILY GOALS	%	%	%	%	%	%

WATER   1 cup per circle
(1 cup = 8 ounces ~ 240ml)   ◯◯◯◯◯◯◯◯◯◯◯◯◯◯◯

DATE: [ ] **WEEK:** [ ] **WEIGHT:** [ ]

Warm Up/ Stretching			**Duration:**	[ ]

Exercise		Set 1	Set 2	Set 3	Set 4	Set 5
	Weight					
	Reps					
	Weight					
	Reps					
	Weight					
	Reps					
	Weight					
	Reps					
	Weight					
	Reps					
	Weight					
	Reps					
	Weight					
	Reps					
	Weight					
	Reps					
	Weight					
	Reps					
	Weight					
	Reps					
	Weight					
	Reps					
	Weight					
	Reps					

CARDIO WORKOUT

Exercise	Duration	Pace	Heart Rate	Calories

Notes:

DAILY CALORIE TARGET: [ ]

BREAKFAST	Protein	Carbs	Fat	Fiber	Sodium	Calories

SNACK	Protein	Carbs	Fat	Fiber	Sodium	Calories

LUNCH	Protein	Carbs	Fat	Fiber	Sodium	Calories

SNACK	Protein	Carbs	Fat	Fiber	Sodium	Calories

DINNER	Protein	Carbs	Fat	Fiber	Sodium	Calories

SNACK	Protein	Carbs	Fat	Fiber	Sodium	Calories

	Protein	Carbs	Fat	Fiber	Sodium	Calories
DAILY TOTALS						
DAILY GOALS						
% DAILY GOALS	%	%	%	%	%	%

WATER   1 cup per circle
(1 cup = 8 ounces ~ 240ml)   ○ ○ ○ ○ ○ ○ ○ ○ ○ ○ ○ ○ ○ ○ ○ ○

DATE: | **WEEK:** | **WEIGHT:**

| Warm Up/ Stretching | | | | **Duration:** | |

Exercise		Set 1	Set 2	Set 3	Set 4	Set 5
	Weight					
	Reps					
	Weight					
	Reps					
	Weight					
	Reps					
	Weight					
	Reps					
	Weight					
	Reps					
	Weight					
	Reps					
	Weight					
	Reps					
	Weight					
	Reps					
	Weight					
	Reps					
	Weight					
	Reps					
	Weight					
	Reps					
	Weight					
	Reps					
	Weight					
	Reps					

CARDIO WORKOUT

Exercise	Duration	Pace	Heart Rate	Calories

Notes:

DAILY CALORIE TARGET: [ ]

BREAKFAST	Protein	Carbs	Fat	Fiber	Sodium	Calories

SNACK	Protein	Carbs	Fat	Fiber	Sodium	Calories

LUNCH	Protein	Carbs	Fat	Fiber	Sodium	Calories

SNACK	Protein	Carbs	Fat	Fiber	Sodium	Calories

DINNER	Protein	Carbs	Fat	Fiber	Sodium	Calories

SNACK	Protein	Carbs	Fat	Fiber	Sodium	Calories

DAILY TOTALS						
DAILY GOALS						
% DAILY GOALS	%	%	%	%	%	%

WATER   1 cup per circle
(1 cup = 8 ounces ~ 240ml)   ○ ○ ○ ○ ○ ○ ○ ○ ○ ○ ○ ○ ○ ○ ○ ○

DATE:	WEEK:	WEIGHT:

Warm Up/ Stretching				Duration:		

Exercise		Set 1	Set 2	Set 3	Set 4	Set 5
	Weight					
	Reps					
	Weight					
	Reps					
	Weight					
	Reps					
	Weight					
	Reps					
	Weight					
	Reps					
	Weight					
	Reps					
	Weight					
	Reps					
	Weight					
	Reps					
	Weight					
	Reps					
	Weight					
	Reps					
	Weight					
	Reps					
	Weight					
	Reps					
	Weight					
	Reps					

CARDIO WORKOUT

Exercise	Duration	Pace	Heart Rate	Calories

Notes:

DAILY CALORIE TARGET:

BREAKFAST	Protein	Carbs	Fat	Fiber	Sodium	Calories

SNACK	Protein	Carbs	Fat	Fiber	Sodium	Calories

LUNCH	Protein	Carbs	Fat	Fiber	Sodium	Calories

SNACK	Protein	Carbs	Fat	Fiber	Sodium	Calories

DINNER	Protein	Carbs	Fat	Fiber	Sodium	Calories

SNACK	Protein	Carbs	Fat	Fiber	Sodium	Calories
DAILY TOTALS						
DAILY GOALS						
% DAILY GOALS	%	%	%	%	%	%

WATER   1 cup per circle
(1 cup = 8 ounces ~ 240ml)   ○○○○○○○○○○○○○○○

DATE: _____ **WEEK:** _____ **WEIGHT:** _____

Warm Up/ Stretching		Duration: _____

Exercise		Set 1	Set 2	Set 3	Set 4	Set 5
	Weight					
	Reps					
	Weight					
	Reps					
	Weight					
	Reps					
	Weight					
	Reps					
	Weight					
	Reps					
	Weight					
	Reps					
	Weight					
	Reps					
	Weight					
	Reps					
	Weight					
	Reps					
	Weight					
	Reps					
	Weight					
	Reps					
	Weight					
	Reps					
	Weight					
	Reps					

CARDIO WORKOUT

Exercise	Duration	Pace	Heart Rate	Calories

Notes:

DAILY CALORIE TARGET:

BREAKFAST	Protein	Carbs	Fat	Fiber	Sodium	Calories

SNACK	Protein	Carbs	Fat	Fiber	Sodium	Calories

LUNCH	Protein	Carbs	Fat	Fiber	Sodium	Calories

SNACK	Protein	Carbs	Fat	Fiber	Sodium	Calories

DINNER	Protein	Carbs	Fat	Fiber	Sodium	Calories

SNACK	Protein	Carbs	Fat	Fiber	Sodium	Calories

DAILY TOTALS						
DAILY GOALS						
% DAILY GOALS	%	%	%	%	%	%

WATER   1 cup per circle
(1 cup = 8 ounces ~ 240ml)   ○○○○○○○○○○○○○○○○

DATE:		WEEK:		WEIGHT:	

Warm Up/ Stretching				Duration:	

Exercise		Set 1	Set 2	Set 3	Set 4	Set 5
	Weight					
	Reps					
	Weight					
	Reps					
	Weight					
	Reps					
	Weight					
	Reps					
	Weight					
	Reps					
	Weight					
	Reps					
	Weight					
	Reps					
	Weight					
	Reps					
	Weight					
	Reps					
	Weight					
	Reps					
	Weight					
	Reps					
	Weight					
	Reps					
	Weight					
	Reps					

CARDIO WORKOUT

Exercise	Duration	Pace	Heart Rate	Calories

Notes:

DAILY CALORIE TARGET: [_____]

BREAKFAST	Protein	Carbs	Fat	Fiber	Sodium	Calories

SNACK	Protein	Carbs	Fat	Fiber	Sodium	Calories

LUNCH	Protein	Carbs	Fat	Fiber	Sodium	Calories

SNACK	Protein	Carbs	Fat	Fiber	Sodium	Calories

DINNER	Protein	Carbs	Fat	Fiber	Sodium	Calories

SNACK	Protein	Carbs	Fat	Fiber	Sodium	Calories

DAILY TOTALS						
DAILY GOALS						
% DAILY GOALS	%	%	%	%	%	%

WATER   1 cup per circle
(1 cup = 8 ounces ~ 240ml)   ◯ ◯ ◯ ◯ ◯ ◯ ◯ ◯ ◯ ◯ ◯ ◯ ◯ ◯ ◯

DATE:		WEEK:		WEIGHT:	

Warm Up/ Stretching					Duration:	

Exercise		Set 1	Set 2	Set 3	Set 4	Set 5
	Weight					
	Reps					
	Weight					
	Reps					
	Weight					
	Reps					
	Weight					
	Reps					
	Weight					
	Reps					
	Weight					
	Reps					
	Weight					
	Reps					
	Weight					
	Reps					
	Weight					
	Reps					
	Weight					
	Reps					
	Weight					
	Reps					
	Weight					
	Reps					
	Weight					
	Reps					

CARDIO WORKOUT

Exercise	Duration	Pace	Heart Rate	Calories

Notes:

DAILY CALORIE TARGET: [   ]

BREAKFAST	Protein	Carbs	Fat	Fiber	Sodium	Calories

SNACK	Protein	Carbs	Fat	Fiber	Sodium	Calories

LUNCH	Protein	Carbs	Fat	Fiber	Sodium	Calories

SNACK	Protein	Carbs	Fat	Fiber	Sodium	Calories

DINNER	Protein	Carbs	Fat	Fiber	Sodium	Calories

SNACK	Protein	Carbs	Fat	Fiber	Sodium	Calories

DAILY TOTALS						
DAILY GOALS						
% DAILY GOALS	%	%	%	%	%	%

WATER   1 cup per circle
(1 cup = 8 ounces ~ 240ml)   ○ ○ ○ ○ ○ ○ ○ ○ ○ ○ ○ ○ ○ ○ ○

DATE:		WEEK:		WEIGHT:	

Warm Up/ Stretching				Duration:	

Exercise		Set 1	Set 2	Set 3	Set 4	Set 5
	Weight					
	Reps					
	Weight					
	Reps					
	Weight					
	Reps					
	Weight					
	Reps					
	Weight					
	Reps					
	Weight					
	Reps					
	Weight					
	Reps					
	Weight					
	Reps					
	Weight					
	Reps					
	Weight					
	Reps					
	Weight					
	Reps					
	Weight					
	Reps					

CARDIO WORKOUT

Exercise	Duration	Pace	Heart Rate	Calories

Notes:

DAILY CALORIE TARGET:

BREAKFAST	Protein	Carbs	Fat	Fiber	Sodium	Calories

SNACK	Protein	Carbs	Fat	Fiber	Sodium	Calories

LUNCH	Protein	Carbs	Fat	Fiber	Sodium	Calories

SNACK	Protein	Carbs	Fat	Fiber	Sodium	Calories

DINNER	Protein	Carbs	Fat	Fiber	Sodium	Calories

SNACK	Protein	Carbs	Fat	Fiber	Sodium	Calories

DAILY TOTALS						
DAILY GOALS						
% DAILY GOALS	%	%	%	%	%	%

WATER   1 cup per circle
(1 cup = 8 ounces ~ 240ml)   ○○○○○○○○○○○○○○○○

DATE:		WEEK:		WEIGHT:	

Warm Up/ Stretching				Duration:	

Exercise		Set 1	Set 2	Set 3	Set 4	Set 5
	Weight					
	Reps					
	Weight					
	Reps					
	Weight					
	Reps					
	Weight					
	Reps					
	Weight					
	Reps					
	Weight					
	Reps					
	Weight					
	Reps					
	Weight					
	Reps					
	Weight					
	Reps					
	Weight					
	Reps					
	Weight					
	Reps					
	Weight					
	Reps					
	Weight					
	Reps					

CARDIO WORKOUT

Exercise	Duration	Pace	Heart Rate	Calories

Notes:

DAILY CALORIE TARGET:

BREAKFAST	Protein	Carbs	Fat	Fiber	Sodium	Calories
SNACK	Protein	Carbs	Fat	Fiber	Sodium	Calories
LUNCH	Protein	Carbs	Fat	Fiber	Sodium	Calories
SNACK	Protein	Carbs	Fat	Fiber	Sodium	Calories
DINNER	Protein	Carbs	Fat	Fiber	Sodium	Calories
SNACK	Protein	Carbs	Fat	Fiber	Sodium	Calories
DAILY TOTALS						
DAILY GOALS						
% DAILY GOALS	%	%	%	%	%	%

WATER   1 cup per circle
(1 cup = 8 ounces ~ 240ml)   ○○○○○○○○○○○○○○○

DATE:		WEEK:		WEIGHT:	

Warm Up/ Stretching	Duration:	

Exercise		Set 1	Set 2	Set 3	Set 4	Set 5
	Weight					
	Reps					
	Weight					
	Reps					
	Weight					
	Reps					
	Weight					
	Reps					
	Weight					
	Reps					
	Weight					
	Reps					
	Weight					
	Reps					
	Weight					
	Reps					
	Weight					
	Reps					
	Weight					
	Reps					
	Weight					
	Reps					
	Weight					
	Reps					
	Weight					
	Reps					

CARDIO WORKOUT

Exercise	Duration	Pace	Heart Rate	Calories

Notes:

DAILY CALORIE TARGET:

BREAKFAST	Protein	Carbs	Fat	Fiber	Sodium	Calories

SNACK	Protein	Carbs	Fat	Fiber	Sodium	Calories

LUNCH	Protein	Carbs	Fat	Fiber	Sodium	Calories

SNACK	Protein	Carbs	Fat	Fiber	Sodium	Calories

DINNER	Protein	Carbs	Fat	Fiber	Sodium	Calories

SNACK	Protein	Carbs	Fat	Fiber	Sodium	Calories

DAILY TOTALS						
DAILY GOALS						
% DAILY GOALS	%	%	%	%	%	%

WATER   1 cup per circle
(1 cup = 8 ounces ~ 240ml)   ○○○○○○○○○○○○○○○○

DATE:		WEEK:		WEIGHT:	

Warm Up/ Stretching				Duration:	

Exercise		Set 1	Set 2	Set 3	Set 4	Set 5
	Weight					
	Reps					
	Weight					
	Reps					
	Weight					
	Reps					
	Weight					
	Reps					
	Weight					
	Reps					
	Weight					
	Reps					
	Weight					
	Reps					
	Weight					
	Reps					
	Weight					
	Reps					
	Weight					
	Reps					
	Weight					
	Reps					
	Weight					
	Reps					
	Weight					
	Reps					

CARDIO WORKOUT

Exercise	Duration	Pace	Heart Rate	Calories

Notes:

DAILY CALORIE TARGET: [ ]

BREAKFAST	Protein	Carbs	Fat	Fiber	Sodium	Calories

SNACK	Protein	Carbs	Fat	Fiber	Sodium	Calories

LUNCH	Protein	Carbs	Fat	Fiber	Sodium	Calories

SNACK	Protein	Carbs	Fat	Fiber	Sodium	Calories

DINNER	Protein	Carbs	Fat	Fiber	Sodium	Calories

SNACK	Protein	Carbs	Fat	Fiber	Sodium	Calories
DAILY TOTALS						
DAILY GOALS						
% DAILY GOALS	%	%	%	%	%	%

WATER   1 cup per circle
(1 cup = 8 ounces ~ 240ml)

○ ○ ○ ○ ○ ○ ○ ○ ○ ○ ○ ○ ○ ○ ○

DATE:		WEEK:		WEIGHT:	

Warm Up/ Stretching				Duration:	

Exercise		Set 1	Set 2	Set 3	Set 4	Set 5
	Weight					
	Reps					
	Weight					
	Reps					
	Weight					
	Reps					
	Weight					
	Reps					
	Weight					
	Reps					
	Weight					
	Reps					
	Weight					
	Reps					
	Weight					
	Reps					
	Weight					
	Reps					
	Weight					
	Reps					
	Weight					
	Reps					
	Weight					
	Reps					
	Weight					
	Reps					

CARDIO WORKOUT

Exercise	Duration	Pace	Heart Rate	Calories

Notes:

DAILY CALORIE TARGET: [   ]

BREAKFAST	Protein	Carbs	Fat	Fiber	Sodium	Calories

SNACK	Protein	Carbs	Fat	Fiber	Sodium	Calories

LUNCH	Protein	Carbs	Fat	Fiber	Sodium	Calories

SNACK	Protein	Carbs	Fat	Fiber	Sodium	Calories

DINNER	Protein	Carbs	Fat	Fiber	Sodium	Calories

SNACK	Protein	Carbs	Fat	Fiber	Sodium	Calories
DAILY TOTALS						
DAILY GOALS						
% DAILY GOALS	%	%	%	%	%	%

WATER   1 cup per circle
(1 cup = 8 ounces ~ 240ml)   ○ ○ ○ ○ ○ ○ ○ ○ ○ ○ ○ ○ ○ ○ ○

DATE:		WEEK:		WEIGHT:	

Warm Up/ Stretching			Duration:	

Exercise		Set 1	Set 2	Set 3	Set 4	Set 5
	Weight					
	Reps					
	Weight					
	Reps					
	Weight					
	Reps					
	Weight					
	Reps					
	Weight					
	Reps					
	Weight					
	Reps					
	Weight					
	Reps					
	Weight					
	Reps					
	Weight					
	Reps					
	Weight					
	Reps					
	Weight					
	Reps					
	Weight					
	Reps					
	Weight					
	Reps					

CARDIO WORKOUT

Exercise	Duration	Pace	Heart Rate	Calories

Notes:

DAILY CALORIE TARGET: [　　　]

BREAKFAST	Protein	Carbs	Fat	Fiber	Sodium	Calories

SNACK	Protein	Carbs	Fat	Fiber	Sodium	Calories

LUNCH	Protein	Carbs	Fat	Fiber	Sodium	Calories

SNACK	Protein	Carbs	Fat	Fiber	Sodium	Calories

DINNER	Protein	Carbs	Fat	Fiber	Sodium	Calories

SNACK	Protein	Carbs	Fat	Fiber	Sodium	Calories

DAILY TOTALS						
DAILY GOALS						
% DAILY GOALS	%	%	%	%	%	%

WATER   1 cup per circle
(1 cup = 8 ounces ~ 240ml)   ○○○○○○○○○○○○○○○

DATE: _____ **WEEK:** _____ **WEIGHT:** _____

Warm Up/ Stretching					Duration:	

Exercise		Set 1	Set 2	Set 3	Set 4	Set 5
	Weight					
	Reps					
	Weight					
	Reps					
	Weight					
	Reps					
	Weight					
	Reps					
	Weight					
	Reps					
	Weight					
	Reps					
	Weight					
	Reps					
	Weight					
	Reps					
	Weight					
	Reps					
	Weight					
	Reps					
	Weight					
	Reps					
	Weight					
	Reps					
	Weight					
	Reps					

CARDIO WORKOUT

Exercise	Duration	Pace	Heart Rate	Calories

Notes:

DAILY CALORIE TARGET: [ ]

BREAKFAST	Protein	Carbs	Fat	Fiber	Sodium	Calories

SNACK	Protein	Carbs	Fat	Fiber	Sodium	Calories

LUNCH	Protein	Carbs	Fat	Fiber	Sodium	Calories

SNACK	Protein	Carbs	Fat	Fiber	Sodium	Calories

DINNER	Protein	Carbs	Fat	Fiber	Sodium	Calories

SNACK	Protein	Carbs	Fat	Fiber	Sodium	Calories
DAILY TOTALS						
DAILY GOALS						
% DAILY GOALS	%	%	%	%	%	%

WATER   1 cup per circle
(1 cup = 8 ounces ~ 240ml)   ○○○○○○○○○○○○○○○○

DATE:		WEEK:		WEIGHT:	

Warm Up/ Stretching Duration:

Exercise		Set 1	Set 2	Set 3	Set 4	Set 5
	Weight					
	Reps					
	Weight					
	Reps					
	Weight					
	Reps					
	Weight					
	Reps					
	Weight					
	Reps					
	Weight					
	Reps					
	Weight					
	Reps					
	Weight					
	Reps					
	Weight					
	Reps					
	Weight					
	Reps					
	Weight					
	Reps					
	Weight					
	Reps					
	Weight					
	Reps					

CARDIO WORKOUT

Exercise	Duration	Pace	Heart Rate	Calories

Notes:

DAILY CALORIE TARGET: [ ]

BREAKFAST	Protein	Carbs	Fat	Fiber	Sodium	Calories

SNACK	Protein	Carbs	Fat	Fiber	Sodium	Calories

LUNCH	Protein	Carbs	Fat	Fiber	Sodium	Calories

SNACK	Protein	Carbs	Fat	Fiber	Sodium	Calories

DINNER	Protein	Carbs	Fat	Fiber	Sodium	Calories

SNACK	Protein	Carbs	Fat	Fiber	Sodium	Calories

DAILY TOTALS						
DAILY GOALS						
% DAILY GOALS	%	%	%	%	%	%

WATER   1 cup per circle
(1 cup = 8 ounces ~ 240ml)   ○○○○○○○○○○○○○○○○

DATE:		WEEK:		WEIGHT:	

Warm Up/ Stretching   **Duration:**

Exercise		Set 1	Set 2	Set 3	Set 4	Set 5
	Weight					
	Reps					
	Weight					
	Reps					
	Weight					
	Reps					
	Weight					
	Reps					
	Weight					
	Reps					
	Weight					
	Reps					
	Weight					
	Reps					
	Weight					
	Reps					
	Weight					
	Reps					
	Weight					
	Reps					
	Weight					
	Reps					
	Weight					
	Reps					

CARDIO WORKOUT

Exercise	Duration	Pace	Heart Rate	Calories

Notes:

DAILY CALORIE TARGET: [ ]

BREAKFAST	Protein	Carbs	Fat	Fiber	Sodium	Calories

SNACK	Protein	Carbs	Fat	Fiber	Sodium	Calories

LUNCH	Protein	Carbs	Fat	Fiber	Sodium	Calories

SNACK	Protein	Carbs	Fat	Fiber	Sodium	Calories

DINNER	Protein	Carbs	Fat	Fiber	Sodium	Calories

SNACK	Protein	Carbs	Fat	Fiber	Sodium	Calories
DAILY TOTALS						
DAILY GOALS						
% DAILY GOALS	%	%	%	%	%	%

WATER   1 cup per circle
(1 cup = 8 ounces ~ 240ml)   ○○○○○○○○○○○○○○○○○

DATE:	WEEK:	WEIGHT:

Warm Up/ Stretching				Duration:	

Exercise		Set 1	Set 2	Set 3	Set 4	Set 5
	Weight					
	Reps					
	Weight					
	Reps					
	Weight					
	Reps					
	Weight					
	Reps					
	Weight					
	Reps					
	Weight					
	Reps					
	Weight					
	Reps					
	Weight					
	Reps					
	Weight					
	Reps					
	Weight					
	Reps					
	Weight					
	Reps					
	Weight					
	Reps					

CARDIO WORKOUT

Exercise	Duration	Pace	Heart Rate	Calories

Notes:

DAILY CALORIE TARGET: [   ]

BREAKFAST	Protein	Carbs	Fat	Fiber	Sodium	Calories

SNACK	Protein	Carbs	Fat	Fiber	Sodium	Calories

LUNCH	Protein	Carbs	Fat	Fiber	Sodium	Calories

SNACK	Protein	Carbs	Fat	Fiber	Sodium	Calories

DINNER	Protein	Carbs	Fat	Fiber	Sodium	Calories

SNACK	Protein	Carbs	Fat	Fiber	Sodium	Calories

DAILY TOTALS						
DAILY GOALS						
% DAILY GOALS	%	%	%	%	%	%

WATER   1 cup per circle
(1 cup = 8 ounces ~ 240ml)   ○ ○ ○ ○ ○ ○ ○ ○ ○ ○ ○ ○ ○ ○ ○ ○

DATE:		WEEK:		WEIGHT:	

Warm Up/ Stretching			Duration:	

Exercise		Set 1	Set 2	Set 3	Set 4	Set 5
	Weight					
	Reps					
	Weight					
	Reps					
	Weight					
	Reps					
	Weight					
	Reps					
	Weight					
	Reps					
	Weight					
	Reps					
	Weight					
	Reps					
	Weight					
	Reps					
	Weight					
	Reps					
	Weight					
	Reps					
	Weight					
	Reps					
	Weight					
	Reps					

CARDIO WORKOUT

Exercise	Duration	Pace	Heart Rate	Calories

Notes:

DAILY CALORIE TARGET: [ ]

BREAKFAST	Protein	Carbs	Fat	Fiber	Sodium	Calories

SNACK	Protein	Carbs	Fat	Fiber	Sodium	Calories

LUNCH	Protein	Carbs	Fat	Fiber	Sodium	Calories

SNACK	Protein	Carbs	Fat	Fiber	Sodium	Calories

DINNER	Protein	Carbs	Fat	Fiber	Sodium	Calories

SNACK	Protein	Carbs	Fat	Fiber	Sodium	Calories

DAILY TOTALS						
DAILY GOALS						
% DAILY GOALS	%	%	%	%	%	%

WATER   1 cup per circle
(1 cup = 8 ounces ~ 240ml)   ◯◯◯◯◯◯◯◯◯◯◯◯◯◯◯

DATE:		WEEK:		WEIGHT:	

Warm Up/ Stretching				Duration:	

Exercise		Set 1	Set 2	Set 3	Set 4	Set 5
	Weight					
	Reps					
	Weight					
	Reps					
	Weight					
	Reps					
	Weight					
	Reps					
	Weight					
	Reps					
	Weight					
	Reps					
	Weight					
	Reps					
	Weight					
	Reps					
	Weight					
	Reps					
	Weight					
	Reps					
	Weight					
	Reps					
	Weight					
	Reps					

CARDIO WORKOUT

Exercise	Duration	Pace	Heart Rate	Calories

Notes:

DAILY CALORIE TARGET:

BREAKFAST	Protein	Carbs	Fat	Fiber	Sodium	Calories

SNACK	Protein	Carbs	Fat	Fiber	Sodium	Calories

LUNCH	Protein	Carbs	Fat	Fiber	Sodium	Calories

SNACK	Protein	Carbs	Fat	Fiber	Sodium	Calories

DINNER	Protein	Carbs	Fat	Fiber	Sodium	Calories

SNACK	Protein	Carbs	Fat	Fiber	Sodium	Calories

DAILY TOTALS						
DAILY GOALS						
% DAILY GOALS	%	%	%	%	%	%

WATER   1 cup per circle
(1 cup = 8 ounces ~ 240ml)   ◯◯◯◯◯◯◯◯◯◯◯◯◯◯◯

DATE: | **WEEK:** | **WEIGHT:**

Warm Up/ Stretching						Duration:

Exercise		Set 1	Set 2	Set 3	Set 4	Set 5
	Weight					
	Reps					
	Weight					
	Reps					
	Weight					
	Reps					
	Weight					
	Reps					
	Weight					
	Reps					
	Weight					
	Reps					
	Weight					
	Reps					
	Weight					
	Reps					
	Weight					
	Reps					
	Weight					
	Reps					
	Weight					
	Reps					
	Weight					
	Reps					
	Weight					
	Reps					

CARDIO WORKOUT

Exercise	Duration	Pace	Heart Rate	Calories

Notes:

DAILY CALORIE TARGET: [   ]

BREAKFAST	Protein	Carbs	Fat	Fiber	Sodium	Calories

SNACK	Protein	Carbs	Fat	Fiber	Sodium	Calories

LUNCH	Protein	Carbs	Fat	Fiber	Sodium	Calories

SNACK	Protein	Carbs	Fat	Fiber	Sodium	Calories

DINNER	Protein	Carbs	Fat	Fiber	Sodium	Calories

SNACK	Protein	Carbs	Fat	Fiber	Sodium	Calories

DAILY TOTALS						
DAILY GOALS						
% DAILY GOALS	%	%	%	%	%	%

WATER   1 cup per circle
(1 cup = 8 ounces ~ 240ml)   ◯ ◯ ◯ ◯ ◯ ◯ ◯ ◯ ◯ ◯ ◯ ◯ ◯ ◯ ◯

DATE:		WEEK:		WEIGHT:	

Warm Up/ Stretching	Duration:

Exercise		Set 1	Set 2	Set 3	Set 4	Set 5
	Weight					
	Reps					
	Weight					
	Reps					
	Weight					
	Reps					
	Weight					
	Reps					
	Weight					
	Reps					
	Weight					
	Reps					
	Weight					
	Reps					
	Weight					
	Reps					
	Weight					
	Reps					
	Weight					
	Reps					
	Weight					
	Reps					
	Weight					
	Reps					

CARDIO WORKOUT

Exercise	Duration	Pace	Heart Rate	Calories

Notes:

DAILY CALORIE TARGET: [   ]

BREAKFAST	Protein	Carbs	Fat	Fiber	Sodium	Calories

SNACK	Protein	Carbs	Fat	Fiber	Sodium	Calories

LUNCH	Protein	Carbs	Fat	Fiber	Sodium	Calories

SNACK	Protein	Carbs	Fat	Fiber	Sodium	Calories

DINNER	Protein	Carbs	Fat	Fiber	Sodium	Calories

SNACK	Protein	Carbs	Fat	Fiber	Sodium	Calories

DAILY TOTALS						
DAILY GOALS						
% DAILY GOALS	%	%	%	%	%	%

WATER   1 cup per circle
(1 cup = 8 ounces ~ 240ml)   ○ ○ ○ ○ ○ ○ ○ ○ ○ ○ ○ ○ ○ ○ ○ ○

DATE:		WEEK:		WEIGHT:	

Warm Up/ Stretching				Duration:	

Exercise		Set 1	Set 2	Set 3	Set 4	Set 5
	Weight					
	Reps					
	Weight					
	Reps					
	Weight					
	Reps					
	Weight					
	Reps					
	Weight					
	Reps					
	Weight					
	Reps					
	Weight					
	Reps					
	Weight					
	Reps					
	Weight					
	Reps					
	Weight					
	Reps					
	Weight					
	Reps					
	Weight					
	Reps					

CARDIO WORKOUT

Exercise	Duration	Pace	Heart Rate	Calories

Notes:

DAILY CALORIE TARGET: _____

BREAKFAST	Protein	Carbs	Fat	Fiber	Sodium	Calories

SNACK	Protein	Carbs	Fat	Fiber	Sodium	Calories

LUNCH	Protein	Carbs	Fat	Fiber	Sodium	Calories

SNACK	Protein	Carbs	Fat	Fiber	Sodium	Calories

DINNER	Protein	Carbs	Fat	Fiber	Sodium	Calories

SNACK	Protein	Carbs	Fat	Fiber	Sodium	Calories

DAILY TOTALS						
DAILY GOALS						
% DAILY GOALS	%	%	%	%	%	%

WATER   1 cup per circle
(1 cup = 8 ounces ~ 240ml)   ○ ○ ○ ○ ○ ○ ○ ○ ○ ○ ○ ○ ○ ○

DATE:		WEEK:		WEIGHT:	

Warm Up/ Stretching				Duration:	

Exercise		Set 1	Set 2	Set 3	Set 4	Set 5
	Weight					
	Reps					
	Weight					
	Reps					
	Weight					
	Reps					
	Weight					
	Reps					
	Weight					
	Reps					
	Weight					
	Reps					
	Weight					
	Reps					
	Weight					
	Reps					
	Weight					
	Reps					
	Weight					
	Reps					
	Weight					
	Reps					
	Weight					
	Reps					

CARDIO WORKOUT

Exercise	Duration	Pace	Heart Rate	Calories

Notes:

DAILY CALORIE TARGET: [   ]

BREAKFAST	Protein	Carbs	Fat	Fiber	Sodium	Calories

SNACK	Protein	Carbs	Fat	Fiber	Sodium	Calories

LUNCH	Protein	Carbs	Fat	Fiber	Sodium	Calories

SNACK	Protein	Carbs	Fat	Fiber	Sodium	Calories

DINNER	Protein	Carbs	Fat	Fiber	Sodium	Calories

SNACK	Protein	Carbs	Fat	Fiber	Sodium	Calories

	Protein	Carbs	Fat	Fiber	Sodium	Calories
DAILY TOTALS						
DAILY GOALS						
% DAILY GOALS	%	%	%	%	%	%

WATER   1 cup per circle
(1 cup = 8 ounces ~ 240ml)   ○ ○ ○ ○ ○ ○ ○ ○ ○ ○ ○ ○ ○ ○ ○

DATE:		WEEK:		WEIGHT:	

Warm Up/ Stretching			Duration:	

Exercise		Set 1	Set 2	Set 3	Set 4	Set 5
	Weight					
	Reps					
	Weight					
	Reps					
	Weight					
	Reps					
	Weight					
	Reps					
	Weight					
	Reps					
	Weight					
	Reps					
	Weight					
	Reps					
	Weight					
	Reps					
	Weight					
	Reps					
	Weight					
	Reps					
	Weight					
	Reps					
	Weight					
	Reps					

CARDIO WORKOUT

Exercise	Duration	Pace	Heart Rate	Calories

Notes:

DAILY CALORIE TARGET:

BREAKFAST	Protein	Carbs	Fat	Fiber	Sodium	Calories

SNACK	Protein	Carbs	Fat	Fiber	Sodium	Calories

LUNCH	Protein	Carbs	Fat	Fiber	Sodium	Calories

SNACK	Protein	Carbs	Fat	Fiber	Sodium	Calories

DINNER	Protein	Carbs	Fat	Fiber	Sodium	Calories

SNACK	Protein	Carbs	Fat	Fiber	Sodium	Calories

DAILY TOTALS						
DAILY GOALS						
% DAILY GOALS	%	%	%	%	%	%

WATER   1 cup per circle
(1 cup = 8 ounces ~ 240ml)   ◯ ◯ ◯ ◯ ◯ ◯ ◯ ◯ ◯ ◯ ◯ ◯ ◯ ◯ ◯

DATE:	WEEK:	WEIGHT:

| Warm Up/ Stretching | | | | Duration: | |

Exercise		Set 1	Set 2	Set 3	Set 4	Set 5
	Weight					
	Reps					
	Weight					
	Reps					
	Weight					
	Reps					
	Weight					
	Reps					
	Weight					
	Reps					
	Weight					
	Reps					
	Weight					
	Reps					
	Weight					
	Reps					
	Weight					
	Reps					
	Weight					
	Reps					
	Weight					
	Reps					
	Weight					
	Reps					

CARDIO WORKOUT

Exercise	Duration	Pace	Heart Rate	Calories

Notes:

DAILY CALORIE TARGET: [   ]

BREAKFAST	Protein	Carbs	Fat	Fiber	Sodium	Calories

SNACK	Protein	Carbs	Fat	Fiber	Sodium	Calories

LUNCH	Protein	Carbs	Fat	Fiber	Sodium	Calories

SNACK	Protein	Carbs	Fat	Fiber	Sodium	Calories

DINNER	Protein	Carbs	Fat	Fiber	Sodium	Calories

SNACK	Protein	Carbs	Fat	Fiber	Sodium	Calories

DAILY TOTALS						
DAILY GOALS						
% DAILY GOALS	%	%	%	%	%	%

WATER   1 cup per circle
(1 cup = 8 ounces ~ 240ml)   ◯◯◯◯◯◯◯◯◯◯◯◯◯◯◯◯◯

DATE:		WEEK:		WEIGHT:	

Warm Up/ Stretching			Duration:	

Exercise		Set 1	Set 2	Set 3	Set 4	Set 5
	Weight					
	Reps					
	Weight					
	Reps					
	Weight					
	Reps					
	Weight					
	Reps					
	Weight					
	Reps					
	Weight					
	Reps					
	Weight					
	Reps					
	Weight					
	Reps					
	Weight					
	Reps					
	Weight					
	Reps					
	Weight					
	Reps					
	Weight					
	Reps					

CARDIO WORKOUT

Exercise	Duration	Pace	Heart Rate	Calories

Notes:

DAILY CALORIE TARGET: [ ]

BREAKFAST	Protein	Carbs	Fat	Fiber	Sodium	Calories

SNACK	Protein	Carbs	Fat	Fiber	Sodium	Calories

LUNCH	Protein	Carbs	Fat	Fiber	Sodium	Calories

SNACK	Protein	Carbs	Fat	Fiber	Sodium	Calories

DINNER	Protein	Carbs	Fat	Fiber	Sodium	Calories

SNACK	Protein	Carbs	Fat	Fiber	Sodium	Calories

DAILY TOTALS						
DAILY GOALS						
% DAILY GOALS	%	%	%	%	%	%

WATER   1 cup per circle
(1 cup = 8 ounces ~ 240ml)   ○ ○ ○ ○ ○ ○ ○ ○ ○ ○ ○ ○ ○ ○ ○ ○

DATE:	WEEK:	WEIGHT:

Warm Up/ Stretching	Duration:

Exercise		Set 1	Set 2	Set 3	Set 4	Set 5
	Weight					
	Reps					
	Weight					
	Reps					
	Weight					
	Reps					
	Weight					
	Reps					
	Weight					
	Reps					
	Weight					
	Reps					
	Weight					
	Reps					
	Weight					
	Reps					
	Weight					
	Reps					
	Weight					
	Reps					
	Weight					
	Reps					
	Weight					
	Reps					

CARDIO WORKOUT

Exercise	Duration	Pace	Heart Rate	Calories

Notes:

DAILY CALORIE TARGET: [   ]

BREAKFAST	Protein	Carbs	Fat	Fiber	Sodium	Calories

SNACK	Protein	Carbs	Fat	Fiber	Sodium	Calories

LUNCH	Protein	Carbs	Fat	Fiber	Sodium	Calories

SNACK	Protein	Carbs	Fat	Fiber	Sodium	Calories

DINNER	Protein	Carbs	Fat	Fiber	Sodium	Calories

SNACK	Protein	Carbs	Fat	Fiber	Sodium	Calories
DAILY TOTALS						
DAILY GOALS						
% DAILY GOALS	%	%	%	%	%	%

WATER   1 cup per circle
(1 cup = 8 ounces ~ 240ml)   ○○○○○○○○○○○○○○○○○○

DATE:		WEEK:		WEIGHT:	

Warm Up/ Stretching			Duration:	

Exercise		Set 1	Set 2	Set 3	Set 4	Set 5
	Weight					
	Reps					
	Weight					
	Reps					
	Weight					
	Reps					
	Weight					
	Reps					
	Weight					
	Reps					
	Weight					
	Reps					
	Weight					
	Reps					
	Weight					
	Reps					
	Weight					
	Reps					
	Weight					
	Reps					
	Weight					
	Reps					
	Weight					
	Reps					
	Weight					
	Reps					

CARDIO WORKOUT

Exercise	Duration	Pace	Heart Rate	Calories

Notes:

DAILY CALORIE TARGET: [ ]

BREAKFAST	Protein	Carbs	Fat	Fiber	Sodium	Calories

SNACK	Protein	Carbs	Fat	Fiber	Sodium	Calories

LUNCH	Protein	Carbs	Fat	Fiber	Sodium	Calories

SNACK	Protein	Carbs	Fat	Fiber	Sodium	Calories

DINNER	Protein	Carbs	Fat	Fiber	Sodium	Calories

SNACK	Protein	Carbs	Fat	Fiber	Sodium	Calories

DAILY TOTALS						
DAILY GOALS						
% DAILY GOALS	%	%	%	%	%	%

WATER   1 cup per circle
(1 cup = 8 ounces ~ 240ml)   ○ ○ ○ ○ ○ ○ ○ ○ ○ ○ ○ ○ ○ ○ ○ ○

DATE:		WEEK:		WEIGHT:	

Warm Up/ Stretching				Duration:	

Exercise		Set 1	Set 2	Set 3	Set 4	Set 5
	Weight					
	Reps					
	Weight					
	Reps					
	Weight					
	Reps					
	Weight					
	Reps					
	Weight					
	Reps					
	Weight					
	Reps					
	Weight					
	Reps					
	Weight					
	Reps					
	Weight					
	Reps					
	Weight					
	Reps					
	Weight					
	Reps					
	Weight					
	Reps					
	Weight					
	Reps					

CARDIO WORKOUT

Exercise	Duration	Pace	Heart Rate	Calories

Notes:

DAILY CALORIE TARGET:

BREAKFAST	Protein	Carbs	Fat	Fiber	Sodium	Calories

SNACK	Protein	Carbs	Fat	Fiber	Sodium	Calories

LUNCH	Protein	Carbs	Fat	Fiber	Sodium	Calories

SNACK	Protein	Carbs	Fat	Fiber	Sodium	Calories

DINNER	Protein	Carbs	Fat	Fiber	Sodium	Calories

SNACK	Protein	Carbs	Fat	Fiber	Sodium	Calories

DAILY TOTALS						
DAILY GOALS						
% DAILY GOALS	%	%	%	%	%	%

WATER   1 cup per circle
(1 cup = 8 ounces ~ 240ml)   ○○○○○○○○○○○○○○○○○○

DATE:		WEEK:		WEIGHT:	

Warm Up/ Stretching				Duration:		

Exercise		Set 1	Set 2	Set 3	Set 4	Set 5
	Weight					
	Reps					
	Weight					
	Reps					
	Weight					
	Reps					
	Weight					
	Reps					
	Weight					
	Reps					
	Weight					
	Reps					
	Weight					
	Reps					
	Weight					
	Reps					
	Weight					
	Reps					
	Weight					
	Reps					
	Weight					
	Reps					
	Weight					
	Reps					

CARDIO WORKOUT

Exercise	Duration	Pace	Heart Rate	Calories

Notes:

DAILY CALORIE TARGET: [____]

BREAKFAST	Protein	Carbs	Fat	Fiber	Sodium	Calories

SNACK	Protein	Carbs	Fat	Fiber	Sodium	Calories

LUNCH	Protein	Carbs	Fat	Fiber	Sodium	Calories

SNACK	Protein	Carbs	Fat	Fiber	Sodium	Calories

DINNER	Protein	Carbs	Fat	Fiber	Sodium	Calories

SNACK	Protein	Carbs	Fat	Fiber	Sodium	Calories

DAILY TOTALS						
DAILY GOALS						
% DAILY GOALS	%	%	%	%	%	%

WATER   1 cup per circle
(1 cup = 8 ounces ~ 240ml)   ○○○○○○○○○○○○○○○○○

DATE:		WEEK:		WEIGHT:	

Warm Up/ Stretching   Duration: [ ]

Exercise		Set 1	Set 2	Set 3	Set 4	Set 5
	Weight					
	Reps					
	Weight					
	Reps					
	Weight					
	Reps					
	Weight					
	Reps					
	Weight					
	Reps					
	Weight					
	Reps					
	Weight					
	Reps					
	Weight					
	Reps					
	Weight					
	Reps					
	Weight					
	Reps					
	Weight					
	Reps					
	Weight					
	Reps					

CARDIO WORKOUT

Exercise	Duration	Pace	Heart Rate	Calories

Notes:

DAILY CALORIE TARGET: [   ]

BREAKFAST	Protein	Carbs	Fat	Fiber	Sodium	Calories

SNACK	Protein	Carbs	Fat	Fiber	Sodium	Calories

LUNCH	Protein	Carbs	Fat	Fiber	Sodium	Calories

SNACK	Protein	Carbs	Fat	Fiber	Sodium	Calories

DINNER	Protein	Carbs	Fat	Fiber	Sodium	Calories

SNACK	Protein	Carbs	Fat	Fiber	Sodium	Calories

DAILY TOTALS						
DAILY GOALS						
% DAILY GOALS	%	%	%	%	%	%

WATER 1 cup per circle
(1 cup = 8 ounces ~ 240ml)   ○○○○○○○○○○○○○○○

DATE:		WEEK:		WEIGHT:	

Warm Up/ Stretching		Duration:	

Exercise		Set 1	Set 2	Set 3	Set 4	Set 5
	Weight					
	Reps					
	Weight					
	Reps					
	Weight					
	Reps					
	Weight					
	Reps					
	Weight					
	Reps					
	Weight					
	Reps					
	Weight					
	Reps					
	Weight					
	Reps					
	Weight					
	Reps					
	Weight					
	Reps					
	Weight					
	Reps					
	Weight					
	Reps					

CARDIO WORKOUT

Exercise	Duration	Pace	Heart Rate	Calories

Notes:

DAILY CALORIE TARGET:

BREAKFAST	Protein	Carbs	Fat	Fiber	Sodium	Calories

SNACK	Protein	Carbs	Fat	Fiber	Sodium	Calories

LUNCH	Protein	Carbs	Fat	Fiber	Sodium	Calories

SNACK	Protein	Carbs	Fat	Fiber	Sodium	Calories

DINNER	Protein	Carbs	Fat	Fiber	Sodium	Calories

SNACK	Protein	Carbs	Fat	Fiber	Sodium	Calories

DAILY TOTALS						
DAILY GOALS						
% DAILY GOALS	%	%	%	%	%	%

WATER   1 cup per circle
(1 cup = 8 ounces ~ 240ml)   ○ ○ ○ ○ ○ ○ ○ ○ ○ ○ ○ ○ ○ ○

DATE:	WEEK:	WEIGHT:

Warm Up/ Stretching	Duration:

Exercise		Set 1	Set 2	Set 3	Set 4	Set 5
	Weight					
	Reps					
	Weight					
	Reps					
	Weight					
	Reps					
	Weight					
	Reps					
	Weight					
	Reps					
	Weight					
	Reps					
	Weight					
	Reps					
	Weight					
	Reps					
	Weight					
	Reps					
	Weight					
	Reps					
	Weight					
	Reps					
	Weight					
	Reps					

CARDIO WORKOUT

Exercise	Duration	Pace	Heart Rate	Calories

Notes:

DAILY CALORIE TARGET: [   ]

BREAKFAST	Protein	Carbs	Fat	Fiber	Sodium	Calories

SNACK	Protein	Carbs	Fat	Fiber	Sodium	Calories

LUNCH	Protein	Carbs	Fat	Fiber	Sodium	Calories

SNACK	Protein	Carbs	Fat	Fiber	Sodium	Calories

DINNER	Protein	Carbs	Fat	Fiber	Sodium	Calories

SNACK	Protein	Carbs	Fat	Fiber	Sodium	Calories

DAILY TOTALS						
DAILY GOALS						
% DAILY GOALS	%	%	%	%	%	%

WATER   1 cup per circle
(1 cup = 8 ounces ~ 240ml)   ○○○○○○○○○○○○○○○○

DATE:		WEEK:		WEIGHT:	

Warm Up/ Stretching   **Duration:** [   ]

Exercise		Set 1	Set 2	Set 3	Set 4	Set 5
	Weight					
	Reps					
	Weight					
	Reps					
	Weight					
	Reps					
	Weight					
	Reps					
	Weight					
	Reps					
	Weight					
	Reps					
	Weight					
	Reps					
	Weight					
	Reps					
	Weight					
	Reps					
	Weight					
	Reps					
	Weight					
	Reps					
	Weight					
	Reps					

CARDIO WORKOUT

Exercise	Duration	Pace	Heart Rate	Calories

Notes:

DAILY CALORIE TARGET: [ ]

BREAKFAST	Protein	Carbs	Fat	Fiber	Sodium	Calories

SNACK	Protein	Carbs	Fat	Fiber	Sodium	Calories

LUNCH	Protein	Carbs	Fat	Fiber	Sodium	Calories

SNACK	Protein	Carbs	Fat	Fiber	Sodium	Calories

DINNER	Protein	Carbs	Fat	Fiber	Sodium	Calories

SNACK	Protein	Carbs	Fat	Fiber	Sodium	Calories

DAILY TOTALS						
DAILY GOALS						
% DAILY GOALS	%	%	%	%	%	%

WATER   1 cup per circle
(1 cup = 8 ounces ~ 240ml)   ○ ○ ○ ○ ○ ○ ○ ○ ○ ○ ○ ○ ○ ○

DATE:	WEEK:	WEIGHT:

Warm Up/ Stretching   Duration:

Exercise		Set 1	Set 2	Set 3	Set 4	Set 5
	Weight					
	Reps					
	Weight					
	Reps					
	Weight					
	Reps					
	Weight					
	Reps					
	Weight					
	Reps					
	Weight					
	Reps					
	Weight					
	Reps					
	Weight					
	Reps					
	Weight					
	Reps					
	Weight					
	Reps					
	Weight					
	Reps					
	Weight					
	Reps					

CARDIO WORKOUT

Exercise	Duration	Pace	Heart Rate	Calories

Notes:

DAILY CALORIE TARGET: [　　　]

BREAKFAST	Protein	Carbs	Fat	Fiber	Sodium	Calories

SNACK	Protein	Carbs	Fat	Fiber	Sodium	Calories

LUNCH	Protein	Carbs	Fat	Fiber	Sodium	Calories

SNACK	Protein	Carbs	Fat	Fiber	Sodium	Calories

DINNER	Protein	Carbs	Fat	Fiber	Sodium	Calories

SNACK	Protein	Carbs	Fat	Fiber	Sodium	Calories

DAILY TOTALS						
DAILY GOALS						
% DAILY GOALS	%	%	%	%	%	%

WATER   1 cup per circle
(1 cup = 8 ounces ~ 240ml)   ◯◯◯◯◯◯◯◯◯◯◯◯◯◯

DATE:		WEEK:		WEIGHT:	

Warm Up/ Stretching	Duration:	

Exercise		Set 1	Set 2	Set 3	Set 4	Set 5
	Weight					
	Reps					
	Weight					
	Reps					
	Weight					
	Reps					
	Weight					
	Reps					
	Weight					
	Reps					
	Weight					
	Reps					
	Weight					
	Reps					
	Weight					
	Reps					
	Weight					
	Reps					
	Weight					
	Reps					
	Weight					
	Reps					
	Weight					
	Reps					

CARDIO WORKOUT

Exercise	Duration	Pace	Heart Rate	Calories

Notes:

DAILY CALORIE TARGET: [ ]

BREAKFAST	Protein	Carbs	Fat	Fiber	Sodium	Calories

SNACK	Protein	Carbs	Fat	Fiber	Sodium	Calories

LUNCH	Protein	Carbs	Fat	Fiber	Sodium	Calories

SNACK	Protein	Carbs	Fat	Fiber	Sodium	Calories

DINNER	Protein	Carbs	Fat	Fiber	Sodium	Calories

SNACK	Protein	Carbs	Fat	Fiber	Sodium	Calories
DAILY TOTALS						
DAILY GOALS						
% DAILY GOALS	%	%	%	%	%	%

WATER   1 cup per circle
(1 cup = 8 ounces ~ 240ml)   ○ ○ ○ ○ ○ ○ ○ ○ ○ ○ ○ ○ ○ ○ ○

DATE:		WEEK:		WEIGHT:	

Warm Up/ Stretching   Duration:

Exercise		Set 1	Set 2	Set 3	Set 4	Set 5
	Weight					
	Reps					
	Weight					
	Reps					
	Weight					
	Reps					
	Weight					
	Reps					
	Weight					
	Reps					
	Weight					
	Reps					
	Weight					
	Reps					
	Weight					
	Reps					
	Weight					
	Reps					
	Weight					
	Reps					
	Weight					
	Reps					
	Weight					
	Reps					

CARDIO WORKOUT

Exercise	Duration	Pace	Heart Rate	Calories

Notes:

DAILY CALORIE TARGET: [   ]

BREAKFAST	Protein	Carbs	Fat	Fiber	Sodium	Calories

SNACK	Protein	Carbs	Fat	Fiber	Sodium	Calories

LUNCH	Protein	Carbs	Fat	Fiber	Sodium	Calories

SNACK	Protein	Carbs	Fat	Fiber	Sodium	Calories

DINNER	Protein	Carbs	Fat	Fiber	Sodium	Calories

SNACK	Protein	Carbs	Fat	Fiber	Sodium	Calories

DAILY TOTALS						
DAILY GOALS						
% DAILY GOALS	%	%	%	%	%	%

WATER   1 cup per circle
(1 cup = 8 ounces ~ 240ml)   ○ ○ ○ ○ ○ ○ ○ ○ ○ ○ ○ ○ ○ ○ ○ ○

DATE:		WEEK:		WEIGHT:	

Warm Up/ Stretching				Duration:	

Exercise		Set 1	Set 2	Set 3	Set 4	Set 5
	Weight					
	Reps					
	Weight					
	Reps					
	Weight					
	Reps					
	Weight					
	Reps					
	Weight					
	Reps					
	Weight					
	Reps					
	Weight					
	Reps					
	Weight					
	Reps					
	Weight					
	Reps					
	Weight					
	Reps					
	Weight					
	Reps					
	Weight					
	Reps					
	Weight					
	Reps					

CARDIO WORKOUT

Exercise	Duration	Pace	Heart Rate	Calories

Notes:

DAILY CALORIE TARGET:

BREAKFAST	Protein	Carbs	Fat	Fiber	Sodium	Calories
SNACK	Protein	Carbs	Fat	Fiber	Sodium	Calories
LUNCH	Protein	Carbs	Fat	Fiber	Sodium	Calories
SNACK	Protein	Carbs	Fat	Fiber	Sodium	Calories
DINNER	Protein	Carbs	Fat	Fiber	Sodium	Calories
SNACK	Protein	Carbs	Fat	Fiber	Sodium	Calories
DAILY TOTALS						
DAILY GOALS						
% DAILY GOALS	%	%	%	%	%	%

WATER 1 cup per circle
(1 cup = 8 ounces ~ 240ml) ○○○○○○○○○○○○○○○

DATE:	WEEK:	WEIGHT:

Warm Up/ Stretching					Duration:			

Exercise		Set 1	Set 2	Set 3	Set 4	Set 5
	Weight					
	Reps					
	Weight					
	Reps					
	Weight					
	Reps					
	Weight					
	Reps					
	Weight					
	Reps					
	Weight					
	Reps					
	Weight					
	Reps					
	Weight					
	Reps					
	Weight					
	Reps					
	Weight					
	Reps					
	Weight					
	Reps					
	Weight					
	Reps					

CARDIO WORKOUT

Exercise	Duration	Pace	Heart Rate	Calories

Notes:

DAILY CALORIE TARGET: [   ]

BREAKFAST	Protein	Carbs	Fat	Fiber	Sodium	Calories
SNACK	**Protein**	**Carbs**	**Fat**	**Fiber**	**Sodium**	**Calories**
LUNCH	**Protein**	**Carbs**	**Fat**	**Fiber**	**Sodium**	**Calories**
SNACK	**Protein**	**Carbs**	**Fat**	**Fiber**	**Sodium**	**Calories**
DINNER	**Protein**	**Carbs**	**Fat**	**Fiber**	**Sodium**	**Calories**
SNACK	**Protein**	**Carbs**	**Fat**	**Fiber**	**Sodium**	**Calories**
DAILY TOTALS						
DAILY GOALS						
% DAILY GOALS	%	%	%	%	%	%

WATER 1 cup per circle
(1 cup = 8 ounces ~ 240ml)   ◯◯◯◯◯◯◯◯◯◯◯◯◯◯

DATE:		WEEK:		WEIGHT:	

Warm Up/ Stretching Duration: [ ]

Exercise		Set 1	Set 2	Set 3	Set 4	Set 5
	Weight					
	Reps					
	Weight					
	Reps					
	Weight					
	Reps					
	Weight					
	Reps					
	Weight					
	Reps					
	Weight					
	Reps					
	Weight					
	Reps					
	Weight					
	Reps					
	Weight					
	Reps					
	Weight					
	Reps					
	Weight					
	Reps					
	Weight					
	Reps					
	Weight					
	Reps					

CARDIO WORKOUT

Exercise	Duration	Pace	Heart Rate	Calories

Notes:

DAILY CALORIE TARGET:

BREAKFAST	Protein	Carbs	Fat	Fiber	Sodium	Calories

SNACK	Protein	Carbs	Fat	Fiber	Sodium	Calories

LUNCH	Protein	Carbs	Fat	Fiber	Sodium	Calories

SNACK	Protein	Carbs	Fat	Fiber	Sodium	Calories

DINNER	Protein	Carbs	Fat	Fiber	Sodium	Calories

SNACK	Protein	Carbs	Fat	Fiber	Sodium	Calories

DAILY TOTALS						
DAILY GOALS						
% DAILY GOALS	%	%	%	%	%	%

WATER   1 cup per circle
(1 cup = 8 ounces ~ 240ml)   ○ ○ ○ ○ ○ ○ ○ ○ ○ ○ ○ ○ ○ ○ ○ ○

DATE:		WEEK:		WEIGHT:	

Warm Up/ Stretching		Duration:	

Exercise		Set 1	Set 2	Set 3	Set 4	Set 5
	Weight					
	Reps					
	Weight					
	Reps					
	Weight					
	Reps					
	Weight					
	Reps					
	Weight					
	Reps					
	Weight					
	Reps					
	Weight					
	Reps					
	Weight					
	Reps					
	Weight					
	Reps					
	Weight					
	Reps					
	Weight					
	Reps					
	Weight					
	Reps					

CARDIO WORKOUT

Exercise	Duration	Pace	Heart Rate	Calories

Notes:

DAILY CALORIE TARGET: [　　　]

BREAKFAST	Protein	Carbs	Fat	Fiber	Sodium	Calories

SNACK	Protein	Carbs	Fat	Fiber	Sodium	Calories

LUNCH	Protein	Carbs	Fat	Fiber	Sodium	Calories

SNACK	Protein	Carbs	Fat	Fiber	Sodium	Calories

DINNER	Protein	Carbs	Fat	Fiber	Sodium	Calories

SNACK	Protein	Carbs	Fat	Fiber	Sodium	Calories

DAILY TOTALS						
DAILY GOALS						
% DAILY GOALS	%	%	%	%	%	%

WATER   1 cup per circle
(1 cup = 8 ounces ~ 240ml)   ○○○○○○○○○○○○○○○

DATE:		WEEK:		WEIGHT:	

Warm Up/ Stretching	Duration:

Exercise		Set 1	Set 2	Set 3	Set 4	Set 5
	Weight					
	Reps					
	Weight					
	Reps					
	Weight					
	Reps					
	Weight					
	Reps					
	Weight					
	Reps					
	Weight					
	Reps					
	Weight					
	Reps					
	Weight					
	Reps					
	Weight					
	Reps					
	Weight					
	Reps					
	Weight					
	Reps					
	Weight					
	Reps					
	Weight					
	Reps					

CARDIO WORKOUT

Exercise	Duration	Pace	Heart Rate	Calories

Notes:

DAILY CALORIE TARGET: [ ]

BREAKFAST	Protein	Carbs	Fat	Fiber	Sodium	Calories

SNACK	Protein	Carbs	Fat	Fiber	Sodium	Calories

LUNCH	Protein	Carbs	Fat	Fiber	Sodium	Calories

SNACK	Protein	Carbs	Fat	Fiber	Sodium	Calories

DINNER	Protein	Carbs	Fat	Fiber	Sodium	Calories

SNACK	Protein	Carbs	Fat	Fiber	Sodium	Calories

DAILY TOTALS						
DAILY GOALS						
% DAILY GOALS	%	%	%	%	%	%

WATER   1 cup per circle
(1 cup = 8 ounces ~ 240ml)   ○○○○○○○○○○○○○○○○

DATE:		WEEK:		WEIGHT:	

Warm Up/ Stretching   **Duration:**

Exercise		Set 1	Set 2	Set 3	Set 4	Set 5
	Weight					
	Reps					
	Weight					
	Reps					
	Weight					
	Reps					
	Weight					
	Reps					
	Weight					
	Reps					
	Weight					
	Reps					
	Weight					
	Reps					
	Weight					
	Reps					
	Weight					
	Reps					
	Weight					
	Reps					
	Weight					
	Reps					
	Weight					
	Reps					

CARDIO WORKOUT

Exercise	Duration	Pace	Heart Rate	Calories

Notes:

DAILY CALORIE TARGET: [　　　]

BREAKFAST	Protein	Carbs	Fat	Fiber	Sodium	Calories

SNACK	Protein	Carbs	Fat	Fiber	Sodium	Calories

LUNCH	Protein	Carbs	Fat	Fiber	Sodium	Calories

SNACK	Protein	Carbs	Fat	Fiber	Sodium	Calories

DINNER	Protein	Carbs	Fat	Fiber	Sodium	Calories

SNACK	Protein	Carbs	Fat	Fiber	Sodium	Calories

DAILY TOTALS						
DAILY GOALS						
% DAILY GOALS	%	%	%	%	%	%

·WATER   1 cup per circle
(1 cup = 8 ounces ~ 240ml)   ○○○○○○○○○○○○○○○

DATE:	WEEK:	WEIGHT:

Warm Up/ Stretching		Duration:

Exercise		Set 1	Set 2	Set 3	Set 4	Set 5
	Weight					
	Reps					
	Weight					
	Reps					
	Weight					
	Reps					
	Weight					
	Reps					
	Weight					
	Reps					
	Weight					
	Reps					
	Weight					
	Reps					
	Weight					
	Reps					
	Weight					
	Reps					
	Weight					
	Reps					
	Weight					
	Reps					
	Weight					
	Reps					
	Weight					
	Reps					

CARDIO WORKOUT

Exercise	Duration	Pace	Heart Rate	Calories

Notes:

DAILY CALORIE TARGET:

BREAKFAST	Protein	Carbs	Fat	Fiber	Sodium	Calories

SNACK	Protein	Carbs	Fat	Fiber	Sodium	Calories

LUNCH	Protein	Carbs	Fat	Fiber	Sodium	Calories

SNACK	Protein	Carbs	Fat	Fiber	Sodium	Calories

DINNER	Protein	Carbs	Fat	Fiber	Sodium	Calories

SNACK	Protein	Carbs	Fat	Fiber	Sodium	Calories

	Protein	Carbs	Fat	Fiber	Sodium	Calories
DAILY TOTALS						
DAILY GOALS						
% DAILY GOALS	%	%	%	%	%	%

WATER   1 cup per circle
(1 cup = 8 ounces ~ 240ml)   ○○○○○○○○○○○○○○○

DATE:		WEEK:		WEIGHT:	

Warm Up/ Stretching	Duration:	

Exercise		Set 1	Set 2	Set 3	Set 4	Set 5
	Weight					
	Reps					
	Weight					
	Reps					
	Weight					
	Reps					
	Weight					
	Reps					
	Weight					
	Reps					
	Weight					
	Reps					
	Weight					
	Reps					
	Weight					
	Reps					
	Weight					
	Reps					
	Weight					
	Reps					
	Weight					
	Reps					
	Weight					
	Reps					

CARDIO WORKOUT

Exercise	Duration	Pace	Heart Rate	Calories

Notes:

DAILY CALORIE TARGET: [   ]

BREAKFAST	Protein	Carbs	Fat	Fiber	Sodium	Calories

SNACK	Protein	Carbs	Fat	Fiber	Sodium	Calories

LUNCH	Protein	Carbs	Fat	Fiber	Sodium	Calories

SNACK	Protein	Carbs	Fat	Fiber	Sodium	Calories

DINNER	Protein	Carbs	Fat	Fiber	Sodium	Calories

SNACK	Protein	Carbs	Fat	Fiber	Sodium	Calories

DAILY TOTALS						
DAILY GOALS						
% DAILY GOALS	%	%	%	%	%	%

WATER 1 cup per circle
(1 cup = 8 ounces ~ 240ml) ○○○○○○○○○○○○○○○

DATE:		WEEK:		WEIGHT:	

Warm Up/ Stretching			Duration:	

Exercise		Set 1	Set 2	Set 3	Set 4	Set 5
	Weight					
	Reps					
	Weight					
	Reps					
	Weight					
	Reps					
	Weight					
	Reps					
	Weight					
	Reps					
	Weight					
	Reps					
	Weight					
	Reps					
	Weight					
	Reps					
	Weight					
	Reps					
	Weight					
	Reps					
	Weight					
	Reps					
	Weight					
	Reps					

CARDIO WORKOUT

Exercise	Duration	Pace	Heart Rate	Calories

Notes:

DAILY CALORIE TARGET: [   ]

BREAKFAST	Protein	Carbs	Fat	Fiber	Sodium	Calories

SNACK	Protein	Carbs	Fat	Fiber	Sodium	Calories

LUNCH	Protein	Carbs	Fat	Fiber	Sodium	Calories

SNACK	Protein	Carbs	Fat	Fiber	Sodium	Calories

DINNER	Protein	Carbs	Fat	Fiber	Sodium	Calories

SNACK	Protein	Carbs	Fat	Fiber	Sodium	Calories

	Protein	Carbs	Fat	Fiber	Sodium	Calories
DAILY TOTALS						
DAILY GOALS						
% DAILY GOALS	%	%	%	%	%	%

WATER   1 cup per circle
(1 cup = 8 ounces ~ 240ml)   ○○○○○○○○○○○○○○○○

DATE:		WEEK:		WEIGHT:	

Warm Up/ Stretching			Duration:	

Exercise		Set 1	Set 2	Set 3	Set 4	Set 5
	Weight					
	Reps					
	Weight					
	Reps					
	Weight					
	Reps					
	Weight					
	Reps					
	Weight					
	Reps					
	Weight					
	Reps					
	Weight					
	Reps					
	Weight					
	Reps					
	Weight					
	Reps					
	Weight					
	Reps					
	Weight					
	Reps					
	Weight					
	Reps					

CARDIO WORKOUT

Exercise	Duration	Pace	Heart Rate	Calories

Notes:

DAILY CALORIE TARGET: [____]

BREAKFAST	Protein	Carbs	Fat	Fiber	Sodium	Calories

SNACK	Protein	Carbs	Fat	Fiber	Sodium	Calories

LUNCH	Protein	Carbs	Fat	Fiber	Sodium	Calories

SNACK	Protein	Carbs	Fat	Fiber	Sodium	Calories

DINNER	Protein	Carbs	Fat	Fiber	Sodium	Calories

SNACK	Protein	Carbs	Fat	Fiber	Sodium	Calories

DAILY TOTALS						
DAILY GOALS						
% DAILY GOALS	%	%	%	%	%	%

WATER   1 cup per circle
(1 cup = 8 ounces ~ 240ml)   ◯◯◯◯◯◯◯◯◯◯◯◯◯◯◯

DATE:		WEEK:		WEIGHT:	

Warm Up/ Stretching   **Duration:**

Exercise		Set 1	Set 2	Set 3	Set 4	Set 5
	Weight					
	Reps					
	Weight					
	Reps					
	Weight					
	Reps					
	Weight					
	Reps					
	Weight					
	Reps					
	Weight					
	Reps					
	Weight					
	Reps					
	Weight					
	Reps					
	Weight					
	Reps					
	Weight					
	Reps					
	Weight					
	Reps					
	Weight					
	Reps					

CARDIO WORKOUT

Exercise	Duration	Pace	Heart Rate	Calories

Notes:

DAILY CALORIE TARGET: [　　　]

BREAKFAST	Protein	Carbs	Fat	Fiber	Sodium	Calories

SNACK	Protein	Carbs	Fat	Fiber	Sodium	Calories

LUNCH	Protein	Carbs	Fat	Fiber	Sodium	Calories

SNACK	Protein	Carbs	Fat	Fiber	Sodium	Calories

DINNER	Protein	Carbs	Fat	Fiber	Sodium	Calories

SNACK	Protein	Carbs	Fat	Fiber	Sodium	Calories

DAILY TOTALS						
DAILY GOALS						
% DAILY GOALS	%	%	%	%	%	%

WATER   1 cup per circle
(1 cup = 8 ounces ~ 240ml)   ○○○○○○○○○○○○○○○○○

DATE: **WEEK:**   **WEIGHT:**

Warm Up/ Stretching						Duration:	

Exercise		Set 1	Set 2	Set 3	Set 4	Set 5
	Weight					
	Reps					
	Weight					
	Reps					
	Weight					
	Reps					
	Weight					
	Reps					
	Weight					
	Reps					
	Weight					
	Reps					
	Weight					
	Reps					
	Weight					
	Reps					
	Weight					
	Reps					
	Weight					
	Reps					
	Weight					
	Reps					
	Weight					
	Reps					

CARDIO WORKOUT

Exercise	Duration	Pace	Heart Rate	Calories

Notes:

DAILY CALORIE TARGET: [ ]

BREAKFAST	Protein	Carbs	Fat	Fiber	Sodium	Calories

SNACK	Protein	Carbs	Fat	Fiber	Sodium	Calories

LUNCH	Protein	Carbs	Fat	Fiber	Sodium	Calories

SNACK	Protein	Carbs	Fat	Fiber	Sodium	Calories

DINNER	Protein	Carbs	Fat	Fiber	Sodium	Calories

SNACK	Protein	Carbs	Fat	Fiber	Sodium	Calories

DAILY TOTALS						
DAILY GOALS						
% DAILY GOALS	%	%	%	%	%	%

WATER   1 cup per circle
(1 cup = 8 ounces ~ 240ml)   ○○○○○○○○○○○○○○○○

DATE:		WEEK:		WEIGHT:	

Warm Up/ Stretching				Duration:	

Exercise		Set 1	Set 2	Set 3	Set 4	Set 5
	Weight					
	Reps					
	Weight					
	Reps					
	Weight					
	Reps					
	Weight					
	Reps					
	Weight					
	Reps					
	Weight					
	Reps					
	Weight					
	Reps					
	Weight					
	Reps					
	Weight					
	Reps					
	Weight					
	Reps					
	Weight					
	Reps					
	Weight					
	Reps					
	Weight					
	Reps					

CARDIO WORKOUT

Exercise	Duration	Pace	Heart Rate	Calories

Notes:

DAILY CALORIE TARGET: _____

BREAKFAST	Protein	Carbs	Fat	Fiber	Sodium	Calories

SNACK	Protein	Carbs	Fat	Fiber	Sodium	Calories

LUNCH	Protein	Carbs	Fat	Fiber	Sodium	Calories

SNACK	Protein	Carbs	Fat	Fiber	Sodium	Calories

DINNER	Protein	Carbs	Fat	Fiber	Sodium	Calories

SNACK	Protein	Carbs	Fat	Fiber	Sodium	Calories

DAILY TOTALS						
DAILY GOALS						
% DAILY GOALS	%	%	%	%	%	%

WATER 1 cup per circle
(1 cup = 8 ounces ~ 240ml)
◯ ◯ ◯ ◯ ◯ ◯ ◯ ◯ ◯ ◯ ◯ ◯ ◯ ◯

DATE:		WEEK:		WEIGHT:	

Warm Up/ Stretching				Duration:	

Exercise		Set 1	Set 2	Set 3	Set 4	Set 5
	Weight					
	Reps					
	Weight					
	Reps					
	Weight					
	Reps					
	Weight					
	Reps					
	Weight					
	Reps					
	Weight					
	Reps					
	Weight					
	Reps					
	Weight					
	Reps					
	Weight					
	Reps					
	Weight					
	Reps					
	Weight					
	Reps					
	Weight					
	Reps					

CARDIO WORKOUT

Exercise	Duration	Pace	Heart Rate	Calories

Notes:

DAILY CALORIE TARGET: [ ]

BREAKFAST	Protein	Carbs	Fat	Fiber	Sodium	Calories

SNACK	Protein	Carbs	Fat	Fiber	Sodium	Calories

LUNCH	Protein	Carbs	Fat	Fiber	Sodium	Calories

SNACK	Protein	Carbs	Fat	Fiber	Sodium	Calories

DINNER	Protein	Carbs	Fat	Fiber	Sodium	Calories

SNACK	Protein	Carbs	Fat	Fiber	Sodium	Calories

	Protein	Carbs	Fat	Fiber	Sodium	Calories
DAILY TOTALS						
DAILY GOALS						
% DAILY GOALS	%	%	%	%	%	%

WATER   1 cup per circle
(1 cup = 8 ounces ~ 240ml)   ○ ○ ○ ○ ○ ○ ○ ○ ○ ○ ○ ○ ○ ○ ○

DATE:		WEEK:		WEIGHT:	

Warm Up/ Stretching	Duration:	

Exercise		Set 1	Set 2	Set 3	Set 4	Set 5
	Weight					
	Reps					
	Weight					
	Reps					
	Weight					
	Reps					
	Weight					
	Reps					
	Weight					
	Reps					
	Weight					
	Reps					
	Weight					
	Reps					
	Weight					
	Reps					
	Weight					
	Reps					
	Weight					
	Reps					
	Weight					
	Reps					
	Weight					
	Reps					

CARDIO WORKOUT

Exercise	Duration	Pace	Heart Rate	Calories

Notes:

DAILY CALORIE TARGET: [ ]

BREAKFAST	Protein	Carbs	Fat	Fiber	Sodium	Calories

SNACK	Protein	Carbs	Fat	Fiber	Sodium	Calories

LUNCH	Protein	Carbs	Fat	Fiber	Sodium	Calories

SNACK	Protein	Carbs	Fat	Fiber	Sodium	Calories

DINNER	Protein	Carbs	Fat	Fiber	Sodium	Calories

SNACK	Protein	Carbs	Fat	Fiber	Sodium	Calories
DAILY TOTALS						
DAILY GOALS						
% DAILY GOALS	%	%	%	%	%	%

WATER   1 cup per circle
(1 cup = 8 ounces ~ 240ml)   ○○○○○○○○○○○○○○○○

DATE:		WEEK:		WEIGHT:	

Warm Up/ Stretching   **Duration:** [   ]

Exercise		Set 1	Set 2	Set 3	Set 4	Set 5
	Weight					
	Reps					
	Weight					
	Reps					
	Weight					
	Reps					
	Weight					
	Reps					
	Weight					
	Reps					
	Weight					
	Reps					
	Weight					
	Reps					
	Weight					
	Reps					
	Weight					
	Reps					
	Weight					
	Reps					
	Weight					
	Reps					
	Weight					
	Reps					

CARDIO WORKOUT

Exercise	Duration	Pace	Heart Rate	Calories

Notes:

DAILY CALORIE TARGET: [ ]

BREAKFAST	Protein	Carbs	Fat	Fiber	Sodium	Calories

SNACK	Protein	Carbs	Fat	Fiber	Sodium	Calories

LUNCH	Protein	Carbs	Fat	Fiber	Sodium	Calories

SNACK	Protein	Carbs	Fat	Fiber	Sodium	Calories

DINNER	Protein	Carbs	Fat	Fiber	Sodium	Calories

SNACK	Protein	Carbs	Fat	Fiber	Sodium	Calories

DAILY TOTALS						
DAILY GOALS						
% DAILY GOALS	%	%	%	%	%	%

WATER   1 cup per circle
(1 cup = 8 ounces ~ 240ml)   ○○○○○○○○○○○○○○○○○

DATE: _____ **WEEK:** _____ **WEIGHT:** _____

Warm Up/ Stretching						**Duration:**

Exercise		Set 1	Set 2	Set 3	Set 4	Set 5
	Weight					
	Reps					
	Weight					
	Reps					
	Weight					
	Reps					
	Weight					
	Reps					
	Weight					
	Reps					
	Weight					
	Reps					
	Weight					
	Reps					
	Weight					
	Reps					
	Weight					
	Reps					
	Weight					
	Reps					
	Weight					
	Reps					
	Weight					
	Reps					

CARDIO WORKOUT

Exercise	Duration	Pace	Heart Rate	Calories

Notes:

DAILY CALORIE TARGET: [   ]

BREAKFAST	Protein	Carbs	Fat	Fiber	Sodium	Calories

SNACK	Protein	Carbs	Fat	Fiber	Sodium	Calories

LUNCH	Protein	Carbs	Fat	Fiber	Sodium	Calories

SNACK	Protein	Carbs	Fat	Fiber	Sodium	Calories

DINNER	Protein	Carbs	Fat	Fiber	Sodium	Calories

SNACK	Protein	Carbs	Fat	Fiber	Sodium	Calories

	Protein	Carbs	Fat	Fiber	Sodium	Calories
DAILY TOTALS						
DAILY GOALS						
% DAILY GOALS	%	%	%	%	%	%

WATER   1 cup per circle
(1 cup = 8 ounces ~ 240ml)   ○○○○○○○○○○○○○○○

DATE:		WEEK:		WEIGHT:	

Warm Up/ Stretching	Duration:	

Exercise		Set 1	Set 2	Set 3	Set 4	Set 5
	Weight					
	Reps					
	Weight					
	Reps					
	Weight					
	Reps					
	Weight					
	Reps					
	Weight					
	Reps					
	Weight					
	Reps					
	Weight					
	Reps					
	Weight					
	Reps					
	Weight					
	Reps					
	Weight					
	Reps					
	Weight					
	Reps					
	Weight					
	Reps					

CARDIO WORKOUT

Exercise	Duration	Pace	Heart Rate	Calories

Notes:

DAILY CALORIE TARGET: [   ]

BREAKFAST	Protein	Carbs	Fat	Fiber	Sodium	Calories

SNACK	Protein	Carbs	Fat	Fiber	Sodium	Calories

LUNCH	Protein	Carbs	Fat	Fiber	Sodium	Calories

SNACK	Protein	Carbs	Fat	Fiber	Sodium	Calories

DINNER	Protein	Carbs	Fat	Fiber	Sodium	Calories

SNACK	Protein	Carbs	Fat	Fiber	Sodium	Calories

	Protein	Carbs	Fat	Fiber	Sodium	Calories
DAILY TOTALS						
DAILY GOALS						
% DAILY GOALS	%	%	%	%	%	%

WATER   1 cup per circle
(1 cup = 8 ounces ~ 240ml)   ○ ○ ○ ○ ○ ○ ○ ○ ○ ○ ○ ○ ○ ○ ○

DATE:	WEEK:	WEIGHT:

Warm Up/ Stretching				Duration:		

Exercise		Set 1	Set 2	Set 3	Set 4	Set 5
	Weight					
	Reps					
	Weight					
	Reps					
	Weight					
	Reps					
	Weight					
	Reps					
	Weight					
	Reps					
	Weight					
	Reps					
	Weight					
	Reps					
	Weight					
	Reps					
	Weight					
	Reps					
	Weight					
	Reps					
	Weight					
	Reps					
	Weight					
	Reps					
	Weight					
	Reps					

CARDIO WORKOUT

Exercise	Duration	Pace	Heart Rate	Calories
Notes:				

DAILY CALORIE TARGET: [   ]

BREAKFAST	Protein	Carbs	Fat	Fiber	Sodium	Calories

SNACK	Protein	Carbs	Fat	Fiber	Sodium	Calories

LUNCH	Protein	Carbs	Fat	Fiber	Sodium	Calories

SNACK	Protein	Carbs	Fat	Fiber	Sodium	Calories

DINNER	Protein	Carbs	Fat	Fiber	Sodium	Calories

SNACK	Protein	Carbs	Fat	Fiber	Sodium	Calories

DAILY TOTALS						
DAILY GOALS						
% DAILY GOALS	%	%	%	%	%	%

WATER   1 cup per circle
(1 cup = 8 ounces ~ 240ml)   ◯◯◯◯◯◯◯◯◯◯◯◯◯◯

DATE:	WEEK:	WEIGHT:

Warm Up/ Stretching		Duration:	

Exercise		Set 1	Set 2	Set 3	Set 4	Set 5
	Weight					
	Reps					
	Weight					
	Reps					
	Weight					
	Reps					
	Weight					
	Reps					
	Weight					
	Reps					
	Weight					
	Reps					
	Weight					
	Reps					
	Weight					
	Reps					
	Weight					
	Reps					
	Weight					
	Reps					
	Weight					
	Reps					
	Weight					
	Reps					
	Weight					
	Reps					

CARDIO WORKOUT

Exercise	Duration	Pace	Heart Rate	Calories

Notes:

DAILY CALORIE TARGET: [   ]

BREAKFAST	Protein	Carbs	Fat	Fiber	Sodium	Calories

SNACK	Protein	Carbs	Fat	Fiber	Sodium	Calories

LUNCH	Protein	Carbs	Fat	Fiber	Sodium	Calories

SNACK	Protein	Carbs	Fat	Fiber	Sodium	Calories

DINNER	Protein	Carbs	Fat	Fiber	Sodium	Calories

SNACK	Protein	Carbs	Fat	Fiber	Sodium	Calories

DAILY TOTALS						
DAILY GOALS						
% DAILY GOALS	%	%	%	%	%	%

WATER   1 cup per circle
(1 cup = 8 ounces ~ 240ml)   ○ ○ ○ ○ ○ ○ ○ ○ ○ ○ ○ ○ ○ ○

DATE:		WEEK:		WEIGHT:	

Warm Up/ Stretching		Duration:	

Exercise		Set 1	Set 2	Set 3	Set 4	Set 5
	Weight					
	Reps					
	Weight					
	Reps					
	Weight					
	Reps					
	Weight					
	Reps					
	Weight					
	Reps					
	Weight					
	Reps					
	Weight					
	Reps					
	Weight					
	Reps					
	Weight					
	Reps					
	Weight					
	Reps					
	Weight					
	Reps					
	Weight					
	Reps					

CARDIO WORKOUT

Exercise	Duration	Pace	Heart Rate	Calories

Notes:

DAILY CALORIE TARGET: [   ]

BREAKFAST	Protein	Carbs	Fat	Fiber	Sodium	Calories

SNACK	Protein	Carbs	Fat	Fiber	Sodium	Calories

LUNCH	Protein	Carbs	Fat	Fiber	Sodium	Calories

SNACK	Protein	Carbs	Fat	Fiber	Sodium	Calories

DINNER	Protein	Carbs	Fat	Fiber	Sodium	Calories

SNACK	Protein	Carbs	Fat	Fiber	Sodium	Calories

DAILY TOTALS						
DAILY GOALS						
% DAILY GOALS	%	%	%	%	%	%

WATER   1 cup per circle
(1 cup = 8 ounces ~ 240ml)   ○○○○○○○○○○○○○○○

DATE:		WEEK:		WEIGHT:	

Warm Up/ Stretching   **Duration:**

Exercise		Set 1	Set 2	Set 3	Set 4	Set 5
	Weight					
	Reps					
	Weight					
	Reps					
	Weight					
	Reps					
	Weight					
	Reps					
	Weight					
	Reps					
	Weight					
	Reps					
	Weight					
	Reps					
	Weight					
	Reps					
	Weight					
	Reps					
	Weight					
	Reps					
	Weight					
	Reps					
	Weight					
	Reps					
	Weight					
	Reps					

CARDIO WORKOUT

Exercise	Duration	Pace	Heart Rate	Calories

Notes:

DAILY CALORIE TARGET: [   ]

BREAKFAST	Protein	Carbs	Fat	Fiber	Sodium	Calories

SNACK	Protein	Carbs	Fat	Fiber	Sodium	Calories

LUNCH	Protein	Carbs	Fat	Fiber	Sodium	Calories

SNACK	Protein	Carbs	Fat	Fiber	Sodium	Calories

DINNER	Protein	Carbs	Fat	Fiber	Sodium	Calories

SNACK	Protein	Carbs	Fat	Fiber	Sodium	Calories

DAILY TOTALS						
DAILY GOALS						
% DAILY GOALS	%	%	%	%	%	%

WATER   1 cup per circle
(1 cup = 8 ounces ~ 240ml)   ○○○○○○○○○○○○○○○○

Made in the USA
Columbia, SC
22 May 2020